STRETCH MY FAITH, LORD

The Book of James

JUANITA PURCELL

REGULAR BAPTIST PRESS
1300 North Meacham Road
Schaumburg, Illinois 60173-4806

STRETCH MY FAITH, LORD
© 1992
Regular Baptist Press
Schaumburg, Illinois
1-800-727-4440

Printed in U. S. A.
All rights reserved

Sixth printing—1999

A Special Thanks

To J. O., my husband, pastor and best friend, who gave helpful comments, corrections, and words of encouragement as I wrote each chapter.

Also to Betty Keefe, a faithful friend, who helped me critique the book. Her insight and comments from a woman's perspective added some special touches.

CONTENTS

Preface 7

Introduction 8

LESSON 1   Trials: The Way to Growth 9

LESSON 2   Don't Give Up; Persevere 17

LESSON 3   Temptations Will Come; Expect Them 23

LESSON 4   Is Your Faith Real or Phony? 31

LESSON 5   Do You Play Favorites? 38

LESSON 6   Faith Demands Evidence 44

LESSON 7   Caution: Tongues out of Control 50

LESSON 8   Do You Pass the Tongue Test? 56

LESSON 9   Causes and Cures for Quarrels 63

LESSON 10   Examine Yourself, Not Others 70

LESSON 11   Stretched Faith Patiently Waits 77

LESSON 12   A Final Look at Afflictions 84

Leader's Guide 91

PREFACE

James is a practical book. It was written to give us a picture of what a mature, balanced, grown-up Christian should be like. James is a glowing collection of truths, arguments, questions, probings, and challenges. It invades every area of our lives and explores every area of our personalities.

In five short chapters James leaps from one subject to another without apology. He touches topics from trials to the tongue, from the use of money to patience, from Bible reading to criticism, from temptation to prayer.

My faith has been stretched as I have dug into the book of James to prepare these lessons. I believe the truths that have challenged me will stretch your faith as well.

INTRODUCTION

As we begin our adventure through the book of James, we need to know a few things at the outset: Who wrote the book? When was it written? To whom was it written? Why was it written?

Who wrote the book?

James is the writer of the book. But which James?

James, the son of Zebedee and brother of John?

James, the son of Alphaeus?

James, the father of Judas the disciple?

James, the half brother of Jesus Christ?

The writer does not identify himself in any way other than "a servant of God and of the Lord Jesus Christ" (James 1:1). James, the half brother of Jesus Christ, is the most likely writer.

James lived in the same home as Jesus (Matthew 13:55), but he did not believe Jesus was the Savior (John 7:5). Jesus appeared to James after the resurrection (1 Corinthians 15:5–7). This was the turning point in James's life; he believed that Jesus truly is the Savior. He shared this with his brothers and later became the leader of the church in Jerusalem (Galatians 2:9).

When was it written?

Bible scholars date the writing of the book about A.D. 45–50. This makes it one of the earliest New Testament epistles.

To whom was it written?

James directly addresses "the twelve tribes which are scattered abroad," and he also calls them "brethren." He is writing to Jews (twelve tribes) and fellow believers (brethren).

Why was it written?

At the time James wrote this book, Rome was the capital of the world. Claudius, the emperor, despised the Jews and persecuted them. Many were homeless; families were separated; Jews were experiencing great misery and suffering. The result? The Jews began to scatter and live a lie.

James wrote to encourage his brethren to stand firm in the midst of their trials. He also reminded them that their trials would help produce spiritual maturity in their lives. He went on to exhort the brethren to live godly lives and told them how this could be accomplished. He drew a vivid picture of what a Christian is like in his speech, actions, feelings, and possessions.

James will stretch our faith to its outer limits.

Trials: The Way to Growth

JAMES 1:1–4

"My brethren, count it all joy when ye fall into divers [various] temptations; knowing this, that the trying of your faith worketh patience" (James 1:2, 3).

The book of James is a letter about the Christian life. Every chapter has valuable lessons, but we will profit from them only as we apply the truths to our lives. As we begin each lesson, let us make sure we are not just hearing the words but that we are *doing* what we hear and learn. "But be ye doers of the word, and not hearers only, deceiving your own selves" (James 1:22).

As we begin this lesson, will you pray this prayer with me? "Lord, when all kinds of trials come rushing into my life, help me not to question Your love. Help me remember that You are 'too good to be unkind and too wise to make a mistake.' Keep me from confusion, O Lord, for the honor of Your name. Amen."

To understand and enjoy this first lesson, read the introduction to this study (p. 8).

Introduction
Read James 1:1.

1. How does James identify himself?

2. Who was raised in the same home with James? Read Matthew 13:55 and 56.

3. James didn't identify himself as the brother of Jesus or as
    the leader of the church at Jerusalem. What does this tell
    you about him?

James used the word "servant" *(doulos)* to prove to us his
attitude of devotion and service to Christ. *Doulos* means "a
bondslave," like the one pictured in Exodus 21:1–6. This bondslave loves and gladly serves his master for life.

4. If you were related to a famous or well-known person, what
    would you be tempted to do?

5. Why do we "name-drop"?

6. James's brothers and sisters in Christ were going through
    "fiery trials" (1 Peter 4:12). Read verse 1 again. Describe
    some of the trials you think they may have faced.

7. What had God predicted would happen to the Jews? Read
    Leviticus 26:33 and Deuteronomy 28:37.

"Do you feel like a member of the scattered tribes of Israel as you look back upon other days when your family circle was unbroken and loved ones were near? Then listen to James' first word: Rejoice! You are a servant of God. You belong to the Lord Jesus Christ. God has written a love letter to you. He sends greetings to you. It is He who tells you to rejoice."[1]

If we are to grow, we need to have the right attitude in our trials.

Read James 1:2.

8. We know the book of James was written to believers, so that means it is also for us today. Verse 2 seems to present an unreasonable request. What is it?

9. How do we usually respond when God allows trials in our lives?

10. What wrong evaluation of ourselves do we display when we ask, "Why is this happening to me?"

"If we value comfort more than character, then trials will upset us. If we value the material and physical more than the spiritual, we will not be able to 'count it all joy.' If we live only for the present and forget the future, then trials will make us bitter, not better."[2]

The key word in "count it all joy" is "count." It is a financial term, and it means "to evaluate."

11. Change "count" to "evaluate," and rewrite James 1:2 in your own words.

12. How do the promises in these verses make it possible to "count it all joy" in difficult circumstances?

Philippians 4:13

Isaiah 40:31

Isaiah 26:3

"Son . . . your present situation is not as difficult as it appears—not if you can see your smallness and My greatness in it. . . . The glory of My power shines brightest in the absence of human help."[3]

---

13. (a) What word in James 1:2 and Isaiah 43:2 implies that all believers will at sometime or another go through trials?

    (b) What trial have you gone through lately?

    (c) Evaluate the trial. What has it done, or is it doing, in your life?

14. What could the words "fall into" indicate?

If we are to grow, our faith must be tested.
Read James 1:3 and 4.

15. If you have access to Bible resource material (such as
    Vine's Expository Dictionary of Biblical Words), look up the
    following words and write a more complete definition of
    each one.

    divers (James 1:2)

    temptations (James 1:2)

    trying (James 1:3)

    worketh (James 1:3)

    patience (James 1:3, 4)

    perfect (James 1:4)

    entire (James 1:4)

16. Reread the definitions of the words you looked up and write James 1:2–4 in your own words.

"God is thinking of perfecting people for glory rather than protecting people from unpleasantness. In fact, He may use the injustice and the unpleasantness as a lesson to lead us further in our relationship with Him."[4]

---

17. Many times we are confused when trials come, and we don't know what God is doing in our lives. What does verse 3 say we can know for sure when trials come?

18. What would happen to our faith if it were never tested?

"The brilliance of gold twice refined, then crafted into exquisite jewelry, is breathtaking indeed. But from the comfort of the jewelry store, no one recalls the heat and pressure, stamping and shaping at the hand of the goldsmith that made it possible. Are you living in the crucible? Then take heart! Something beautiful is about to happen at the hands of your Creator."[5]

---

19. When patience has finished its "perfect work," what kind of Christians should we be?

20. (a) Does "wanting [lacking] nothing" in verse 4 relate to material or spiritual things?

    (b) What does this verse mean?

 *From My Heart*

Have you ever noticed how the Lord often tests us to see if we're practicing what we're preaching? The week I started this book, the Lord sent a test that seemed to be the capstone of three years of trials. Needless to say, I was discouraged. I was disappointed and felt like quitting. I was tired and near the point of exhaustion. Late into the night I questioned the Lord and felt so sorry for myself. Then just as if the Lord turned on a light, the darkness and questioning left, and I remembered the lesson I had written on James 1:1–4. As I lay there in bed, this poem began to develop in my mind.

> Lord, will these pains and trials never end?
> Just when I think it's over, another You send.
> You know my heart—how it hurts so bad;
> I'm trying to smile, but I feel so sad.
> What from these trials do You want me to know?
> Oh, I remember; You want me to grow.
> Yes, more like Jesus You want me to be;
> That's the plan You have in mind for me.
> So keep on chipping and banging away;
> Don't stop 'till You're finished, no matter what I say.

From Your Heart

Reflecting over this lesson, have you come to the realization your trials are custom-made by God to help you grow spiritually? What is God trying to teach you in your present trial?

Notes:
1. S. Maxwell Coder, *Faith That Works* (Chicago: Moody Bible Institute, n.d.), p. 4.
2. Warren W. Wiersbe, *Be Mature* (Wheaton, IL: SP Publications, 1978), p. 23.
3. Charles Slagle, *From the Father's Heart* (Shippensburg, PA: Destiny Image Publishers, 1989), p. 84.
4. Stuart Briscoe, *What Works When Life Doesn't* (Wheaton, IL: SP Publications, 1976), p. 136.
5. *Timeless Insights* (Atlanta: Thru the Bible Ministries), August 1990.

Don't Give Up; Persevere
JAMES 1:5–12

"If any of you lack wisdom, let him ask of God, that giveth to all men liberally, and upbraideth not; and it shall be given him"
(James 1:5).

We have learned trials will come to all believers who are striving for spiritual maturity. We need assistance and divine guidance as we endure these trials. I am happy to announce it is available to those who ask for it. If it is that easy, why doesn't everyone have it? We will find out in this lesson.

As we begin this lesson, will you pray this prayer with me? "Lord, when I'm confused / And don't know what to do, / Help me to remember / To run to You. / Others may confuse / Or lead astray, / Only You have the answer / To guide my way. Amen."

Need help? Don't give up; ask for it!
Read James 1:5.

1. What are two things we need when we're in the midst of a trial (verses 5, 6–8)?

2. Why do you think James lists wisdom as the first thing we need when we're being tested?

The word "ask" in James 1:5 is in the present active tense: present tense—ask; active tense—keep asking. This implies to me we need to ask and keep asking and keep waiting for the answer.

3. To whom do we often turn first for wisdom and answers?

4. We may need a pastor or counselor, but to Whom should we go first? Read Isaiah 9:6.

I once heard someone say, "When in trouble, when in doubt, Run in circles, scream and shout." I think this formula would be more practical:
   1. Get on your knees—James 1:5
   2. Get into the Word—2 Timothy 2:15
   3. Get counsel from others—Proverbs 1:5

"Not until we have become humble and teachable, standing in awe of God's holiness and sovereignty ... acknowledging our own littleness, distrusting our own thoughts, and willing to have our minds turned upside down, can divine wisdom become ours."[1]

5 God promises to give His wisdom to us. (a) In what manner will He give it?

(b) What does this mean to you?

6. What does "upbraideth not" mean?

> *"'My times are in thy hand . . .' has become a part of my life. When the Lord has left me in an agony of waiting over some decision, these words have put me at rest. His timing is always perfect, though it seldom seems so to me, for my temperament longs for previews of coming attractions."*[2]

Need faith? Don't give up; dig for it!
Read James 1:6–8.

7. Why is it that some people don't get the wisdom they need from God (verses 6 and 7)?

8. How does God describe a man who lacks faith (verse 6)?

9. Why is a double mind an unstable mind?

> *"It is not hard . . . to trust the management of the universe . . . to the Lord. Can your case be so much more complex and difficult . . . that you need to be anxious or troubled about His management of you? . . . Take your stand on the power and trustworthiness of your God, and see how quickly all difficulties will vanish before a steadfast determination to believe."*[3]

10. How does faith come to a person? Read Romans 10:17.

11. Read Hebrews 11:1. What is your definition of faith?

---

*"You will never learn faith in comfortable sur-
roundings. God gives us the promises in a quiet hour;
God seals our covenants with great and gracious
words, then He steps back and waits to see how
much we believe; then He lets the tempter come, and
the test seems to contradict all that He has spoken.
It is then that faith wins its crown. That is the time to
look up through the storm, and among the trembling,
frightened seamen cry, 'I believe God that it shall be
even as it was told me.'"[4]*

Don't give up; everyone can have true riches!
Read James 1:9–11.

No matter where we are in life—rich, poor, or in between—we will have trials, and we need God's wisdom and
faith as we move from one trial to another.

12. Keep in mind that James was writing to his Christian
    brothers, poor Christians and rich ones. How are they
    alike when trials come?

    (a) The poor

    (b) The rich

---

*"The believer's wealth can never be calculated in
dollars. We are rich in peace, righteousness, and
hope; and neither adversity nor ill-health can take
such wealth away from us."[5]*

---

13. How does verse 11 relate to this world's goods?

You didn't give up; you'll be rewarded.
Read James 1:12.

The word "temptation" in verse 12 is the same word as "divers temptations" or various trials in verse 2.

14. What two things do we find in the life of the blessed person?

"Other things being equal, the attribute that makes a champion is endurance. He keeps on going, sometimes after all the indications are that he is licked. He just won't quit."[6]

---

15. How is the blessed person rewarded for enduring trials?

16. Do you think the "crown of life" refers to a rich, full life now (John 10:10) or a "crown of life" in Heaven for faithful devotion to Christ while on earth (Revelation 2:10)?

 *From My Heart*

Do you remember to ask for wisdom when you're being tested? Most of the time I do, but my biggest problem is waiting for the answer. If God doesn't give me some clear direction or a quick solution, my tendency is to take matters into my own hands. I decide I will try to solve things—or at least help God out a little. This is where I make a big mistake, and God says, "Let not that man think he shall receive any thing of the Lord." If I am going to work things out myself, then God can't do it for me.

Recently I saw a note on someone's refrigerator; it caught my attention. I came home and wrote the same note, and I see it every day on my refrigerator. It says,

Dear Juanita,
I do not need your help today!
Love,
God

"Lord, You know I don't want to be a double-minded person; help me to have an unwavering faith."

From Your Heart

Reflecting over this lesson, do you think God would see you as a champion or a quitter in your present circumstances of life? What is your desire?

Notes:

1. J. I. Packer, quoted by John Blanchard, compiler, *Gathered Gold* (Durham, England: Evangelical Press, 1984), p. 334.

2. Elisabeth Elliot, *Discipline: The Glad Surrender* (Old Tappan, NJ: Fleming H. Revell Co., 1982), p. 101.

3. Hannah Whitall Smith, *The Christian's Secret of a Happy Life* (Westwood, NJ: Fleming H. Revell Co., 1952), p. 76.

4. Mrs. Charles E. Cowman, *Streams in the Desert* (Grand Rapids: Zondervan Publishing House, 1965), p. 11.

5. Lehman Strauss, *James, Your Brother* (Neptune, NJ: Loizeaux Brothers, 1956), p. 30.

6. Ethel Barrett, *Will the Real Phony Please Stand Up* (Glendale, CA: G/L Publications, 1969), p. 7.

Temptations Will Come; Expect Them

JAMES 1:13–21

"Every man is tempted, when he is drawn away of his own lust, and enticed" (James 1:14).

We have learned in lessons 1 and 2 that God sends trials to test and mature our faith. In this lesson we will discover that with every trial there is a temptation. Satan will tempt us to run away from our trial and blame God for our hurt.

God sends tests. What for? So we can bear up and trust God. Satan sends temptations. What for? So we will run away and blame God.

As we begin this lesson, will you pray this prayer with me? "Lord, When I'm faced with a powerful temptation, help me to resist immediately. May I be swift to deny self and quick to follow You. Amen."

"When our circumstances are difficult, we may find ourselves complaining against God, questioning His love, and resisting His will. At this point, Satan provides us with an opportunity to escape the difficulty. This opportunity is a temptation."[1]

We will be tempted to sin.
Read James 1:13–16.

1. What word do we see in verse 13 that indicates we will all be tempted?

2. We've all heard people say, "The Devil made me do it." Why can't we blame God, others, or even Satan for our sin?

3. We think of sin as an act, but God sees it as a progression with at least four stages. Name them.

   (1)

   (2)

   (3)

   (4)

4. The end result of sin is death. James was not speaking of physical death, for his readers were still alive. He was not speaking of spiritual death, for his readers were believers, and believers cannot lose their salvation (John 3:16). What does die as a result of sin?

5. Write in your own words the process involved from lust to death as described in verses 13–16.

   When the inward lust is joined with the outward temptation, sin is born. Who is the unmentioned father? Satan, the great deceiver! He whispers to us, "You don't have to take this; you can get away with this, and no one else will ever know or get hurt."

"Satan does not hand you the temptation with a blueprint showing the frustration, the failure, the alienation from God, the unrealized goals, the drug rehabilitation center, the unwanted pregnancy or whatever *the end might be. He suggests only the pleasure of the moment—and it is implicit that somehow you are going to get away with it and come out unscathed."*[2]

6. Can you think of a time in your life when you sinned after a long period of trials, saying, "I just couldn't take it any longer"? Briefly write what happened to you and what temptation Satan offered as a way to escape.

When we resist what God is allowing in our lives, we are tempted to run away from it rather than accept it. When we run away, we will be tempted to sin; but when we accept it, we find peace. Amy Carmichael beautifully expressed this thought in this poem:

He said, "I will forget the dying faces;
The empty places,
They shall be filled again.
O voices moaning deep within me, cease."
But vain the word; vain, vain:
Not in forgetting lieth peace.

He said, "I will crowd action upon action,
The strife of faction
Shall stir me and sustain;
O tears that drown the fire of manhood, cease."
But vain the word; vain, vain:
Not in endeavor lieth peace.

He said, "I will withdraw me and be quiet,
Why meddle in life's riot?
Shut be my door to pain.
Desire, thou dost befool me, thou shalt cease."
But vain the word; vain, vain:
Not in aloofness lieth peace.

He said, "I will submit; I am defeated.
God hath depleted
My life of its rich gain.
O futile murmurings, why will ye not cease?"
But vain the word; vain, vain:
Not in submission lieth peace.

He said, "I will accept the breaking sorrow
Which God tomorrow
Will to His son explain."
Then did the turmoil deep within him cease.
Not vain the word, not vain;
For in Acceptance lieth peace.[3]

We will be tempted to forget God.
Read James 1:17 and 18.

7. How can remembering the goodness of God keep us from yielding to temptation (verse 17)?

8. Shadows from the sun shift, but not the God Who made the sun. What does this tell you about God?

"Child, All I do, I do in your best interest. In fact, I love you so much that I often look beyond your small requests and give you far better gifts than you ask Me to give." [4]

---

9. What word in verse 18 speaks of birth?

10. What did God use to stimulate new birth in us?

11. (a) Are we begotten or given new life because we choose it or earn it?

    (b) Who originates the new birth, and how is it originated?

12. What did "firstfruits" mean to the Jewish people to whom James was writing?

13. How does God compare those who have been born again to the rest of His creation?

14. If Christians are to be the finest God has to show off to the world, how should that affect our thinking when we are tempted to sin?

We will be tempted to forget God's Word.
Read James 1:19–21.

When we are enticed to sin, we often forget how good God is and that He has saved us to be examples of Christ to this world. We may also forget His Word.

15. Why should we be swift to hear the Word of truth (verse 19)?

16. What does "swift to hear, slow to speak, slow to wrath" have to do with our proneness to sin?

> *"Lord, deliver me from the urge to open my mouth when I should shut it. Give me the wisdom to keep silence where silence is wise. Remind me that not everything needs to be said, and that there are very few things that need to be said* by me." [5]

Remember, anger is one letter short of danger!

17. How does man's anger hinder God's work? Give an illustration you have observed.

> *"I have no more right as a Christian to allow a bad temper to dwell in me than I have to allow the devil himself to dwell there."* [6]

18. How are we to prepare our hearts for the Word of God?

19. What is the significance of the word "engrafted"?

The Greek word for "save" in verse 21 means "to protect, deliver, heal."

20. How does God's Word save our souls?

The Bible will keep me from sin, or sin will keep me from the Bible.

From My Heart

Pulling weeds is one of my least favorite things to do. However, those ugly things have taught me a good lesson about life and my sin. One day as I was weeding, I came across a weed, hidden behind a bush, that was really hard to get out. As I got up to give it a hard tug, I began to reason, "It doesn't look that bad; in fact, it's pretty with those little orange flowers on it. Besides, I might hurt my back if I start tugging on it." So I left it. A month later when I was weeding, I was shocked when I saw my little weed. It was no longer hidden. It was now as big as the bush in front of it. I tugged and pulled, and it didn't budge. I had to get my husband to get it out.

That little weed is like my sin when it first begins to grow in my heart. I reason in my mind, "It isn't that bad." So it grows; and when I decide to do something about it, I can't; the roots are too deep. I need help to get it out. The Great Physician, my Savior, is there to cut it out. However, I must remember, the deeper the roots, the bigger the scar will be.

"Lord, help me to confess my sins daily, so little sins can't grow."

From Your Heart

Reflecting over this lesson, what little sins do you see beginning to take root in your heart? What are you going to do about them?

Notes:

1. Wiersbe, p. 35.

2. Barrett, p. 24.

3. Amy Carmichael, quoted by Elisabeth Elliot, *Loneliness* (Nashville:Thomas Nelson, Inc., Publishers, 1988), pp. 84, 85.

4. Slagle, p. 121.

5. Elisabeth Elliot, *A Lamp for My Feet* (Ann Arbor, MI: Servant Publications, 1985), p. 42.

6. Charles Spurgeon, quoted by Tom Carter, compiler, *Spurgeon at His Best* (Grand Rapids: Baker Book House, 1988), p. 12.

Is Your Faith Real or Phony?

JAMES 1:22–27

"But be ye doers of the word, and not hearers only, deceiving your own selves" (James 1:22).

In the first three lessons we learned how we are to endure trials and overcome temptations. Now it appears as though James is saying, "It's exam time! I want you to examine your faith to see if it is real."

As we begin this lesson, will you pray this prayer with me? "Lord, keep reminding me to check myself regularly to make sure my outward performance and my inward obedience match up. I don't want only to look right; I want to be right! I could easily be deceived. Help me to stay alert for Your name's sake. Amen."

Living faith demands action.
Read James 1:22.

The word "deceiving" in this verse is from a verb that is used only twice in the New Testament: here and in Colossians 2:4. *Paralogizomai* means to "cheat" or "deceive by false reasoning."

1. What is to be our guide in examining our faith to see if it is real?

2. How is God's Word unlike any other book we read?

3. In what way is God's Word a double guide to reality?

4. If a person hears the Word without putting it into practice, how does he deceive himself? Read Matthew 7:24–27.

"Warning: This Book is habit-forming. Regular use causes loss of anxiety, and decreased appetite for lying, cheating, stealing, hating. Symptoms: increased sensations of love, peace, joy, and compassion."[1]

The word "hearer" refers to "an academic auditor." This person hears all the material and takes notes but has no assignments or tests.

5. If God is making no assignments in our lives and never testing us, what should that tell us?

Living faith demands attention.
Read James 1:23 and 24.

6. Like a mirror, what does the Word of God do for us?

7. How do ladies often make it obvious they put more emphasis on outward beauty than on inward beauty?

"Our friends may tell us we are wonderful, and we may even fool ourselves into believing it. We can dream up thousands of ways of improving our own self-image, but when we read the Word of God we see ourselves exactly as we are! It is impossible to be indifferent to the Bible. You may hear it and choose to do nothing about it, but the Bible will do something to you. Truth heard and ignored is dangerous."[2]

---

8. What would we say about a lady who got up in the morning, looked into the mirror at her messy hair, and did not comb it?

Living faith demands obedience.
Read James 1:25.

9. The "law of liberty" refers to the teachings of Christ.
   (a) How does God's Word bring liberty into our lives?

   (b) How could a Christian put himself into bondage?

"Lord, break the chains that hold me to myself; free me to be your happy slave—that is, to be the happy foot-washer of anyone today who needs his feet washed, his supper cooked, his faults overlooked, his work commended, his failure forgiven, his griefs consoled, or his button sewed on. Let me not imagine that my love for you is very great if I am unwilling to do for a human being something very small."[3]

---

10. Who is the "unblessed" person?

11. (a) On an average, how many times a week do you hear
         God's Word, either through your reading or hearing it
         taught?

     (b) What did you do this week that was a result of what
         you heard from God's Word?

12. What do you think this statement means: "Some people go
     through the motions of devotions"?

Living faith demands example.
Read James 1:26 and 27.

13. Verse 26 is a vivid example of a hearer and not a doer.
     (a) A word in this verse indicates this person may not be
         a true believer. What is it?

     (b) What other word or phrase could you use in place of
         "seem"?

14. What does "religious" mean?

15. Why does God use the words "religious" and "religion" when referring to the man in verse 26?

16. What three things are said about this man?

> *"Religion is mankind's attempt to work its way to heaven; Christianity is God's good news that heaven is a free gift. Religion involves trying; Christianity involves relying."* [1]

17. How does vain religion deceive a person? Read 1 Samuel 15:22 and Amos 5:21 and 22.

> *"Our word religion comes from an old Latin root meaning 'taboo.' It may be defined therefore as keeping the taboos, or performing ceremonies and observing customs considered to be sacred. A person can be very religious without ever having heard God's plan of salvation."* [5]

18. What three tests of true faith (pure and undefiled) can we use to discover if our outward service pleases God?

    (1)

(2)

(3)

19. How do we evidence true faith in these three areas?

Bridled tongue

Love for others

Holiness or purity

> *"To know Christ is the way to grow in holiness. Christianity is not a religion of rules. It is the religion of the divine example. Try to follow the blessed steps of the most holy life. Take His advice. Ask yourself, in the moment of perplexity or temptation, what would He do if He were here? Nothing else will so surely lead us into the way of holy living."*[6]

Examine your faith: is it a real faith or a deceived faith? Real faith is not deceived!

 From My Heart

I've chosen James 1:22 as my verse for the year: "Be ye doers of the word, and not hearers only, deceiving your own selves." I don't just want to read the Word of God each day, teach it and hear it taught; I want to *live* it. It is so easy to get into habits that can deceive us. We read our Bibles each day and never miss a church service, but our hearts are filled with anger, hatred and bitterness, fear and worry. What good does it do to read our Bibles each day and never miss a service if we don't obey what we read and hear?

I like this thought I once read: "Why is it that we, in the very kingdom of grace, surrounded by angels and preceded by saints, nevertheless can do so little, and instead of mounting with wings like eagles, grovel in the dust and do but sin and confess sin alternately? We do have a power within us to do what we are commanded to do. What is it we lack? The power? No; the will."

"Yes, I have Your power in me, Lord, but I must keep fanning the flame and rekindling the fire by daily times in Your Word." I must ask myself each day, "Have you added a log to the fire today, Juanita?"

"Lord, You know I want to grow and glow for You and be a hearer and a doer."

What about you?

From Your Heart

Reflecting over this lesson, would you say you have real faith or deceived faith? What evidence of real faith are you demonstrating in your life right now?

Notes:

1. Charles U. Wagner, *Winning Words for Daily Living* (Grand Rapids: Kregel Publications, 1989), p. 50.

2. George Sweeting, *How to Solve Conflicts* (Chicago: Moody Press, 1973), p. 47.

3. Elisabeth Elliot, *A Lamp for My Feet,* pp. 35, 36.

4. *Timeless Insights* (Atlanta: Thru the Bible Ministries), February 1991.

5. Coder, p. 18.

6. George Hodges, quoted by Mary Wilder Tileston, compiler, *Joy and Strength* (Minneapolis: World Wide Publications, 1986), p. 122.

LESSON 5

Do You Play Favorites?

JAMES 2:1–13

"But if ye have respect to persons, ye commit sin, and are convinced [convicted] of the law as transgressors" (James 2:9).

Let us take a quick review of the first chapter of James before we start into the second chapter. We learned four practical lessons in the first chapter:

- God sends trials to mature us.
- We need wisdom and faith to endure trials.
- We will all face temptations.
- God wants us to be "doers" of His Word and "not hearers only."

As we look into chapter 2, we immediately face this question: Can true faith and favoritism be compatible? James strongly implies no! James was obviously upset with his Christian brothers because of the inconsistencies in their faith. They were being partial to certain people and showing favoritism or respect of persons.

The Jews had a tendency to worship wealth. In some synagogues, the scribes and the rabbis had special seats, "chief seats" (Matthew 23:6). The Jews also liked to be saluted in public and were known by the clothing they wore (Mark 12:38). In those days the rich were very rich and had all the rights; the poor were very poor and had no rights. Interestingly enough, in our day of equal rights, this situation still prevails in some parts of the world.

As we begin our lesson, will you pray this prayer with me? "Lord, help me to see people the way You see them, looking beyond the outward appearance and seeing the heart. I cry with the psalmist, 'Open thou mine eyes.' Teach me and lead me, dear Lord. Amen."

How favoritism is displayed
Read James 2:1–7.

1. What does it mean to show "respect of persons"?

2. Why are faith and favoritism not compatible for believers in the glorious Lord Jesus Christ? Read Hebrews 11:1.

"Two strangers arrive. One is clearly wealthy, as he is dressed in 'fine clothes' and is also wearing 'a gold ring.' Some translations have 'gold rings,' which may well be right, as the original Greek word— chrusodaktulios—literally means 'gold-fingered.' He had a gem at every joint, a nugget on every knuckle! The other man was just as plainly poor; not only is that very word used of him, but his shabby clothing bears it out. What a contrast these visitors presented—one in rings and the other in rags!"[1]

---

3. Describe what is happening in verses 2–4 and relate it to a situation that could occur in a church today.

"Is a jewel less precious because it comes in a plain box? Is a person less important when bound up with what we judge to be a limited mind or an unattractive outward appearance?"[2]

---

4. Are we pressured by status symbols? If so, how?

5. What evil thoughts or motives could we have in showing special attention to the rich?

6. (a) Is James implying that the poor will be the only ones who will be heirs of Heaven?

   (b) What is he implying? Read 1 Corinthians 1:26 and 27.

"Lady Huntingdon, the gospel-loving friend of the Wesleys, used to say that she was saved by an 'm,' for, said she, if 1 Corinthians 1:26 had read 'not any wise, not any noble are called,' then she would not have been saved. But it does not read 'not any,' but 'not many.'"[3]

---

7. James wanted the believers to see that favoring the rich and insulting or despising the poor were wrong and totally unreasonable. What three questions did he ask in verses 6 and 7?

   (1)

   (2)

   (3)

How favoritism is denounced
Read James 2:8–13.

   James has proven to the people that favoritism is unreasonable. Now he states that it is sin.

8. We could sum up verses 8 and 9 by saying:

Showing love is _____ _____ .

Having respect of persons is _____ _____.

9. (a) Was the "royal law" a new law to these people?

(b) Why? Read Leviticus 19:18.

10. How does the "royal law" compare to the Ten Commandments in Exodus 20:1–17?

11. Why is "love thy neighbour as thyself" called the "royal law"?

"Hatred makes a person a slave, but love sets us free from selfishness and enables us to reign like kings. Love enables us to obey the Word of God and treat people as God commands us to do."[4]

12. What does verse 10 mean to you?

13. Respect of persons is not a minor mistake. We must look at
     the seriousness of it. James compares it with two ugly sins
     mentioned in verse 11. What are they?

14. How does the "law of liberty" set us free?

---

*"Christian love does not mean that I must like a
person and agree with him on everything. I may not
like his vocabulary or his habits, and I may not want
him for an intimate friend.* Christian love means
treating others the way God has treated me."[5]

---

15. What do verses 12 and 13 mean?

16. Have you ever murdered a person or committed adultery?
     You may be a bit offended even to be asked such a
     question. Let me ask another, "Do you show favoritism or
     respect of persons?" If this has been a problem in your life,
     would you claim 1 John 1:9 and begin to make some
     changes?

17. If we are honest with ourselves, we must admit we sin in
     this area. Give some examples of how we do this in our
     everyday lives.

 *From My Heart*

As I studied this lesson, I had to keep asking myself, "Am I prejudiced in regard to certain people, races, or classes of people?" I didn't think I was until I began to analyze my attitudes and actions. The longer I studied this lesson, the more convicted I felt. I do show respect of persons, maybe not intentionally, but I do.

Maybe you, like me, never realized what an offense this is to God: it is sin! Unconsciously, you and I often categorize sins. We have big sins and little sins. Gossip would be a little sin, murder a big sin; respect of persons would be a little sin, adultery a big sin. God says disobeying His Word (breaking the law) is sin; none of it is little to Him. Only as I give mercy will I receive it. I once read, "Mercy is a song with many verses, but the chorus is hummed softly to yourself." Now I know why I don't always have a song in my heart.

 *From Your Heart*

Reflecting over this lesson, do you know of a person in your life to whom you have been unmerciful and to whom you need to show mercy? What are you going to do about it?

Notes:

1. John Blanchard, *Truth for Life* (Hertfordshire, England: Evangelical Press, 1986), p. 118.

2. Blanchard, p. 118.

3. G. Coleman Luck, *James: Christian Faith in Action* (Chicago: Moody Press, 1954), p. 46.

4. Wiersbe, p. 70.

5. Wiersbe, p. 70.

Faith Demands Evidence

JAMES 2:14–26

"For as the body without the spirit is dead, so faith without works is dead also" (James 2:26).

In our last lesson we learned that practicing the "royal law" gives us no excuse for respect of persons. In this lesson we will learn that possession of faith gives us no excuse to be without good works.

As we begin this lesson, will you pray this prayer with me? "Lord, help me always to remember I am saved by faith plus nothing. Help me also to remember that I am Your workmanship created to do good works. In Your mercy allow me to be used. Do with me as You desire. Amen."

Professing faith

Read James 2:14.

1. What is the difference between saving faith and professing faith?

2. Are we saved by faith or works? Read Ephesians 2:8 and 9.

3. Why do some people think they will go to Heaven as a result of their good works? Read Matthew 7:21–23.

*"It is an awful hypocrisy that declares with the lips
what it denies with the life."[1]*

4. Since we are saved by faith and not by works, what part do
   works have in a believer's life? Read Ephesians 2:10.

   The phrase "though a man say he hath faith" is significant
in understanding the following verses. This man claims something with no supporting evidence. He has nothing to prove
that what he is saying is true.

5. What kind of faith is James referring to in verse 14 when he
   says "can faith save him"?

Dead faith
Read James 2:15–20.

   In verse 15 the word "naked" is from the Greek word
gymnos, which can also mean "poorly clothed."

6. (a) Is God telling us we are responsible to take care of
       every needy person we know of?

   (b) What is He saying?

7. When a plant or a tree is alive, what are some natural
   things that will happen?

8. How does a person demonstrate he has a dead faith
   (verses 17 and 18)?

"Workless faith is worthless faith; it is unproductive, sterile, barren, dead! Great claims may be made about a corpse that is supposed to have come to life, but if it does not move, if there are no vital signs, no heartbeat, no perceptible pulse, it is still dead. The false claims are silenced by the evidence."[2]

---

9. (a) Is there any other real evidence to prove we are Christians other than the lives we live?

   (b) If so, what?

10. In verse 18 James contends that words alone are not enough to prove we are saved. Why not?

"Good works cannot save you [Titus] (3:5), but the absence of good works can effectively negate what you claim to possess [Titus] (1:16). . . . People may be fooled for a time by your profession, but God is never fooled. Without the proper knowledge of Him, 'all our righteousnesses are like filthy rags' (Isaiah 64:6)."[3]

---

11. Anyone can say he believes in Christ. Whom did James cite as an example of this?

   The term "demons," or "devils," has its roots in the Greek word for "intelligence." James said even demons understand God. Their theology is right. They know the facts, and the facts make them fearful; but their belief profits them nothing. Their so-called faith is not saving faith, and it is not associated with deeds of true faith.

12. What do demons believe?

    Mark 3:11

    Luke 8:29–31 (The word "deep" in this verse is the same word as "bottomless pit" in Revelation 20:1–3.)

13. How would you describe a "vain man"?

"The proof of religious conversion is to demonstrate that we have both added a relationship with Christ and that we have subtracted sin (repentance). And we multiply proof to a weary world by what we do— our deeds, our obedience. What we do must confirm what we say. Our deeds are the proof of our repentance. Are you proving your repentance to the world by your deeds?"[4]

Living faith
Read James 2:21–26.

James seems to say, "I'm going to end my message with two illustrations to prove my point."

14. Carefully read verses 21–24. Was Abraham justified (made right with God) by faith plus works or by faith that works?

15. (a) Was Abraham justified when he offered his son Isaac? Read Genesis 15:4–6.

(b) Did he sacrifice Isaac? Read Genesis 22:6–13.

(c) What was Abraham's work of faith? Read Hebrews 11:19.

16. Why would God use a harlot to illustrate living faith? (You can read Rahab's story in Joshua 2:1–22; 6:21–25.)

17. Verses 24–26 could be misunderstood. Someone might get the idea that we are saved by our good works. Why do we know this is not true? Read Ephesians 2:8 and 9.

18. The Bible never contradicts itself. What is James saying in these verses? (Verse 26 is the summary.)

Maybe you need to check your vital signs to see if you are alive spiritually. Would you take a few minutes and take this brief spiritual checkup?
• Was there a time when you honestly realized you were a sinner and asked Christ to save you? When did that take place?
• What changes have taken place in your life since then?
• How are you seeking to grow in the things of Christ?
• What work can be seen by others that is evidence of your spiritual life?

"Say not that thou hast royal blood in thy veins, and art born of God, except thou canst prove thy pedigree by daring to be holy." [5]

From My Heart

Have you ever felt like a nobody and thought, "What can I do for Christ?" I have! I remember when my husband told me God was calling him into the ministry. I said, "No way! You'll be a preacher over my dead body." Why such a reaction? Because I couldn't sing, play the piano, teach, or even pray in public. After five years of struggling with God, I finally realized all He was asking of me was to be yielded and faithful and He would do the rest. I said, "Okay, Lord, I have nothing to offer You, but if there is anything about my life You can use, here it is; use it as You choose."

I often share with ladies that Ephesians 2:10 is a testimony of my life. This is my version of that verse: "I am His workmanship, created in Christ Jesus, to do good works." If there is anything about my life that Christ can use, it is because of His workmanship in molding and transforming me.

"Lord, help me always to remember I am saved by faith plus nothing. But since I am Your workmanship, I am saved to serve."

From Your Heart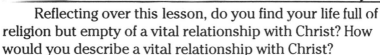

Reflecting over this lesson, do you find your life full of religion but empty of a vital relationship with Christ? How would you describe a vital relationship with Christ?

Notes:

1. Vance Havner, *Day by Day* (Old Tappan, NJ: Fleming H. Revell Co., 1953), p. 212.

2. John F. Walvoord and Roy B. Zuck, eds., *The Bible Knowledge Commentary,* New Testament edition (Wheaton, IL: SP Publications, 1983), p. 825.

3. *Timeless Insights* (Atlanta: Walk Thru the Bible Ministries), June 1991.

4. Patrick M. Morley, *I Surrender* (Brentwood, TN: Wolgemuth & Hyatt, Publishers, Inc., 1990), p. 15.

5. William Gurnall, quoted by Blanchard, *Truth for Life,* p. 175.

Caution: Tongues out of Control

JAMES 3:1–8

---

*"And the tongue is a fire, a world of iniquity: so is the tongue
among our members, that it defileth the whole body . . ."
(James 3:6).*

In chapter 2 James wrote about worthless faith. He now
takes an entire chapter to discuss the damage caused by
worthless, careless words.

Do you ever think of your tongue in terms of a ship's
rudder or a bit in a horse's mouth or a raging fire out of control? Today we will look at the tremendous power of this
seemingly insignificant instrument, the tongue.

As we begin this lesson, will you pray this prayer with me?
"Lord, what an awesome thought to realize I carry in my mouth
an instrument so powerful! I can destroy a person's reputation
and credibility with just a few sharp blasts or save another
from suicide or total despair by one gentle wisp. Teach me to
walk in the Spirit each day so my tongue can be an instrument
of peace, not destruction. Forgive me when I fail. Amen."

The tongue is petite but powerful.

Read James 3:1–5.

1. Why does James give this warning to teachers (verse 1)?
   Read Proverbs 18:21.

2. How do we know we will never be mature enough in our faith never to offend or stumble with our words? Read 1 Corinthians 10:12.

3. How can we tell we are making spiritual progress in regard to our tongues?

"It once was the practice of family physicians as they checked the health of their patients to say, 'Let me look at your tongue.' One glance helped to tell them whether sickness was present. James says to the Christian, 'Let me see your tongue,' and this 'little member' reveals the state of our spiritual health."[1]

---

4. How does James illustrate the power of small things in verses 3 and 4?

5. How is the tongue like a bit and a rudder?

6. How does the tongue control the whole body?

7. How does the tongue control other people?

8. James has not yet identified the tongue as good or evil, just powerful. Describe some incidents you know of where the tongue had the power to influence people for good or evil.

   Good

   Evil

> A careless word may kindle strife;
> A cruel word may wreck a life.
> A bitter word may hate instill;
> A brutal word may smite and kill.
> A gracious word may smooth the way;
> A joyous word may light the day.
> A timely word may lessen stress;
> A loving word may heal and bless.[2]

9. Why is the tongue compared to fire in verse 5?

10. Can you think of an incident when someone's tongue did inestimable damage? What was it?

11. Has your tongue ever crushed or devastated a person? Have you gone to the person and asked for forgiveness? Why must you do this? Read Matthew 5:23 and 24.

The tongue is treacherous and untamable.

Read James 3:6–8.

12. James now likens the tongue to a "world of iniquity," or evil. What does that say about the tongue?

13. How may the tongue defile the whole body (verse 6)? Read Matthew 15:11 and 18–20 and Mark 7:15.

14. Can you think of an example in your life or in the life of another when an uncontrolled tongue defiled a person?

"And setteth on fire the course of nature" is a difficult phrase. The word "course" is the Greek *trochos*, which means "wheel." The wheel was an ancient symbol of the whole cycle of life from birth to death. This verse seems to say that there is not only no part of life that the tongue cannot affect, but there is no time in life when it cannot be affected as well.

15. (a) Does time (or getting older) correct the sins of the tongue (verse 6)?

    (b) Why?

16. Fire can be tamed, and animals can be tamed. Why can't we tame our tongues (verses 7 and 8)?

> *"I am more deadly than the screaming shell from the howitzer. I win without killing. I tear down homes, break hearts, and wreck lives. I travel on the wings of the wind. No innocence is strong enough to intimidate me, no purity pure enough to daunt me. I have no regard for truth, no respect for justice, no mercy for the defenseless. My victims are as numerous as the sands of the sea, and often as innocent. I never forget and seldom forgive. My name is Gossip."[3]*

17. The untamable tongue is described as an "unruly evil, full of deadly poison." Why are these descriptions accurate?

    Unruly evil

    Full of deadly poison

> *"One of the first things that happens when a man is really filled with the Spirit is not that he speaks with tongues, but that he learns to hold the one tongue he already has."[4]*

18. Since we cannot control what we say, Who can help us? Read Psalm 141:3.

 *From My Heart*

Have you ever had someone come to you and just pour out her heart? I have. The person's life is filled with turmoil and problems. She needs help, and she is looking to me for the answers. It is almost frightening to realize she is going to do whatever I tell her because she doesn't know what else to do.

My words have the power to save her from utter defeat—or make things worse. It is imperative I walk close to Christ each day so I can be guided by His Spirit as I talk to people. I never know what hour of the day or night my doorbell or phone will ring with a cry for help.

"Lord, remind me daily to cleanse my tongue with the Word so it can be an instrument of peace."

From Your Heart

Reflecting over this lesson, have you come to grips with how damaging an uncontrolled tongue can be? What steps are you going to take to tame your tongue?

Notes:
1. Coder, p. 2.
2. Unknown author, quoted by J. Vernon McGee, *Thru the Bible with J. Vernon McGee* (Nashville: Thomas Nelson, Inc., Publishers, 1983), vol. 5, p. 655.
3. Morgan Blake, quoted by Sweeting, p. 77.
4. J. Sidlow Baxter, quoted by Blanchard, *Gathered Gold,* p. 299.

LESSON 8

Do You Pass the Tongue Test?

JAMES 3:9–18

"Out of the same mouth proceedeth blessing and cursing. My brethren, these things ought not so to be" (James 3:10).

In James 2 we learned to test our faith by our works. In James 3 we will test our faith by our tongues. We will ask, and seek to answer, three questions in this lesson to see if we pass the tongue test.
- Do I speak with a forked tongue?
- Does my tongue demonstrate earthly, sensual, devilish wisdom?
- Does my tongue demonstrate heavenly wisdom?

As we begin this study, will you pray this prayer with me? "Lord, take control of my life and remind me each day to seek the wisdom that is from above. I want the words of my mouth and the meditations of my heart to be acceptable in Your sight (Psalm 19:14). Only then will they be acceptable to others. Grant my request, dear Lord. Amen."

Do I speak with a forked tongue?
Read James 3:9–13.

1. An old Indian saying goes, "He speaks with a forked tongue." What does this mean?

2. How could someone curse another person if he did not use what is called "curse words" (verse 9)?

56

> *"The other day I heard someone say, 'The Christian army is the only army in the world that kills its wounded.' . . . The very people who have the most potential to be kind and loving can also be the most cruel and judgmental."[1]*

3. If we pray a curse on another person, what does this reveal about us? Read 1 John 4:20 and 21.

4. What is a hypocrite?

> *"Ananias and Sapphira pretended to be something they were not [Acts 5:1–10]. God might not judge hypocrisy in a believer's life quite as dramatically as He did in the early church, but any form of pretense leads to death—of faith, relationships, and a desire to serve."[2]*

5. How does loving God and hating men picture hypocrisy (verses 12 and 13)?

6. What is the key to making sure only blessings and not cursing flow from our mouths? Read John 3:16 and Galatians 5:16 and 17.

Does my tongue demonstrate earthly, sensual, devilish wisdom?
Read James 3:14–16.

James now contrasts the tongue of the unwise and wise believer.

7. What indicators show up in a person's life to let him know his wisdom is not from God (verse 14)?

"Before you flare up at any one's faults, take time to count ten—ten of your own."[3]

---

8. How do "glory not, and lie not against the truth" (verse 14) relate to envy and strife?

9. What is another word for envy?

10. How is jealousy a twin to strife?

11. Define these terms that describe worldly wisdom:

    earthly

    sensual

    devilish

12. What is the end result of envy and strife (verse 16)?

13. How can we know that confusion and disorder in our lives are the result of worldly wisdom? Read 1 Corinthians 14:33.

"When we use worldly wisdom in trying to do God's work, when we use nothing more than our own natural ingenuity to gain our ends or settle arguments in our favour, the end result is uncannily disappointing, and not only does it come to nothing on earth, but it will lead to nothing in heaven, because it will be among those things that will be 'burned up' (1 Co- rinthians 3:15). The wisdom that comes from hell will get us nowhere in heaven!"[4]

Does my tongue demonstrate heavenly wisdom?
Read James 3:13, 17, and 18.

We have seen a vivid picture of worldly (counterfeit) wisdom. We will now see James's description of heavenly (real) wisdom.

14. Why can true wisdom be called a good and perfect gift (James 1:17)?

15. "Good conversation" in verse 13 can be translated "good life." How do we show others we are living a good life?

Some say "gentleness" would be a good word to use in describing "meekness," yet it is a particular kind of gentleness. It is a quality that accepts without retaliation the insults and injuries caused by others, recognizing that these, too, are under God's sovereign control.

16. When we want a true picture of this kind of gentleness and meekness, to Whom should we look? Read 2 Corinthians 10:1.

17. How did Christ demonstrate gentleness according to 1 Peter 2:21–23?

"Paul's enemies wounded him with stones; there is a wounding with words even worse than stones. . . . And what had Paul done that he deserved to be stoned? He was bringing men and women away from error, and bringing them to God—benefits worthy of crowns, not of stones. Has one insulted you? Hold your peace, and bless if you can. Then you also will have preached the Word, and given a lesson of gentleness and meekness."[5]

---

18. Verse 17 describes heavenly wisdom. If you have a Bible dictionary or other resource materials, look up the following words and write their definitions, telling how each word applies to the tongue.

Pure

Peaceable

Gentle

Easy to be entreated

Full of mercy

Good fruits

Without partiality

Without hypocrisy

Did you pass the tongue test? Do you speak with heavenly wisdom?

19. (a) Read again the definition of God's wisdom in verse 17. How would you rate yourself on a scale of 1 to 10, with 10 being the best?

1 2 3 4 5 6 7 8 9 10

(b) When and where is it the hardest for you to show this kind of wisdom?

20. Whatever we sow we reap (Galatians 6:7). How can we have peace in our lives (verse 18)?

Do you sow peace with your words, or do you tend to be critical and picky? If you have difficulty being a peacemaker, it might be well for you to read this prayer by Francis of Assisi. After reading it, ask God to make it a reality in your life.

> "Lord, make me an instrument of your peace.
> Where there is hatred, let me sow love;
> Where there is injury, pardon;
> Where there is doubt, faith;
> Where there is despair, hope;
> Where there is darkness, light;
> Where there is sadness, joy."

From My Heart

Have you ever been on a diet? I am probably getting one of two answers: "I'm always on a diet," or "No; I need to gain weight." It seems very few of us can hit that happy medium and stay there without working at it. Yes, diets and exercise programs are a common way of life for many of us who don't want to keep enlarging our dress size.

Have you ever thought about being on a "word diet"? I had never even heard of such a thing until recently. Let me share it with you. A word diet is like a food diet, cutting down on how much you eat and limiting food to nonfattening and nutritious items. Likewise, a word diet involves cutting down on the quantity of your words and improving the quality of words. Sounds pretty good. I think I had better try it. How about you?

Someone gave me this little poem when I was teaching on the tongue: "Lord, fill my mouth with worthwhile stuff, And nudge me when I've said enough."

"Keep nudging me, Lord!"

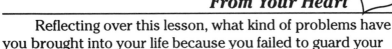

From Your Heart

Reflecting over this lesson, what kind of problems have you brought into your life because you failed to guard your tongue? Memorize Proverbs 21:23 this week.

Notes:

1. Morgan McKenzie, quoted by Barbara Johnson, *Fresh Elastic for Stretched Out Moms* (Old Tappan, NJ: Fleming H. Revell Co., 1986), p. 118.

2. *Timeless Insights* (Atlanta: Thru the Bible Ministries), February 1991.

3. Jo Perry, compiler, *Apples of Gold* (Norwalk, CT: The C. R. Gibson Co., 1962), p. 45.

4. Blanchard, *Truth for Life*, p. 215.

5. John Chrysostom, quoted in *Timeless Insights*, February 1991.

LESSON 9

Causes and Cures for Quarrels

JAMES 4:1–7

"Submit yourselves therefore to God. Resist the devil, and he will flee from you" (James 4:7).

James 3 ends with these comforting words: "The fruit of righteousness is sown in peace of them that make peace." Now James takes a sharp turn. Chapter 4 opens with "wars and fightings." Usually when James starts a new subject, he begins with "my brethren"; but not this time. Could it be he is speaking in a different tone of voice? James seems to be stirred and upset with the conflicts going on in the lives of the brethren.

The old nature has not changed in two thousand years. We still face the same causes and cures for conflicts and quarrels. We will look at the causes, consequences, and cures for quarrels in this lesson.

As we begin, will you pray this prayer with me? "Lord, my old nature is my constant enemy, always ready to raise its ugly head to destroy me. Empower me, as I seek Your face, to become more like You and get what I need from You to overcome the sins of the flesh. Thanks for reminding me to 'resist the devil, and he will flee' from me. Amen."

The cause of quarrels
Read James 4:1 and 2.

1. What does "wars and fightings" in verse 1 imply?

2. What is the underlying cause of conflicts and quarrels (verse 1)?

3. On what are you and I generally inclined to blame our quarrels?

4. How does war in people's hearts cause war in homes and churches?

"We are often like a glass of water which has been standing still for hours and looks very clear and bright. But there is a sediment, and a little stir soon discovers it and clouds the crystal. That sediment is the old nature."[1]

---

5. (a) You want something and cannot have it, so you kill to get it. You want something and cannot have it, so you fight and quarrel to get it. What one word can we put over verse 2 to describe the problem at hand?

   (b) How do you demonstrate self-will in your life?

6. How can a Christian kill another person without a gun?

7. (a) Of what are conflicts and quarrels a sign? Read 1 Corinthians 3:3.

   (b) What signs of worldliness (carnality) are in your life?

8. When our hearts are filled with selfish lust, life becomes a vicious circle of seeking but never being satisfied. What are two reasons for this in verses 2 and 3?

9. When people are quarreling, why don't they pray?

> Oh, what peace we often forfeit,
> Oh, what needless pain we bear,
> All because we do not carry
> Everything to God in prayer!

The consequences of quarrels
Read James 4:3–5.

10. If quarrelers do happen to pray, what kind of prayer is it (verse 3)?

11. I heard about this method to check prayers: Tell God why you want it and how you intend to use it. How could this help you avoid asking "amiss"?

12. What is the overruling condition for answered prayer?
    Read 1 John 5:14.

> Thy will, not mine, O Lord,
> However dark it be!
> Lead me by Thine own hand,
> Choose out the path for me.
> I dare not choose my lot;
> I would not, if I might;
> Choose Thou for me, my God;
> So shall I walk aright.[2]

13. (a) How did James address his readers in verse 4?

    (b) What does this tell you about their behavior?

14. What indications do we have in verse 4 that James was
    speaking to the people described in James 3:14–16?

15. Why is friendship with the world considered spiritual
    adultery? Read 2 Corinthians 11:2 and 3.

16. An unfaithful mate leaves his partner to fulfill the lust of
    the flesh with another partner. How does a believer
    demonstrate unfaithfulness to Christ?

> *"Jesus did not pray that his Father would take Christians out of the world, but that he would take the world out of Christians."[3]*

Verse 5 is one of the most difficult verses in James. It may mean the Spirit, Who indwells believers, jealously yearns for us and He gives more grace (verse 6). Or it may mean that the human spirit in people yearns to envy, but God gives more grace.

The cure for quarrels
Read James 4:6 and 7.

17. (a) What is grace?

    (b) To whom is it given (verse 6)?

18. If we are too proud to humble ourselves and admit our sin and need for grace, what will God do to us?

19. If we are caught in the grip of worldliness, what must we do to be set free?

> *"Conformity to the world can be overcome by nothing but conformity to Jesus."[4]*

20. (a) What does it mean to resist the Devil?

(b) How do we do this? Read Ephesians 6:13–17.

> *"I often laugh at Satan, and there is nothing that makes him so angry as when I attack him to his face, and tell him that through God I am more than a match for him."*[5]

 *From My Heart*
_____

Satan is my enemy. He would love to deceive me into believing I am living for God when actually I am slowly becoming more and more like the world instead of more like Christ. I must ask God daily to search my heart and "see if there be any wicked way in me" (Psalm 139:23, 24). Frederick W. Faber expressed this thought so well:

> One thing alone, dear Lord! I dread;—
> To have a secret spot
> That separates my soul from Thee,
> And yet to know it not.[6]

This world is not an easy environment in which to become Christlike, but because "He giveth more grace," it is possible. Whatever besets me, His grace is sufficient to see me through it.

> He giveth more grace when the burdens grow greater,
> He sendeth more strength when the labors increase;
> To added affliction He addeth His mercy,
> To multiplied trials, His multiplied peace.[7]

What a wonderful gift God has given us, His grace—love in action.

From Your Heart
_____

Reflecting over this lesson, is self-will causing conflicts in your life? What is God trying to do in your life to root this out?

Notes:

1. Charles Spurgeon, quoted by Carter, p. 131.
2. Horatius Bonar, quoted by Tileston, p. 87.
3. Blanchard, *Gathered Gold,* p. 337.
4. Andrew Murray, quoted by Blanchard, *Gathered Gold,* p. 338.
5. Martin Luther, quoted by Carter, p. 58.
6. Frederick W. Faber, quoted by Tileston, p. 244.
7. Annie Johnson Flint, quoted by Al Bryant, compiler, *Favorite Poems* (Grand Rapids: Zondervan Publishing House, 1957), p. 68.

Examine Yourself, Not Others

JAMES 4:8–17

"Draw nigh to God, and he will draw nigh to you . . ."
(James 4:8).

In the previous lesson we saw two instructions for those caught in the grip of worldliness: submit to God and resist the Devil. James gives six more admonitions to believers. He tells how to get back on track and how to stay there.

Before we start this lesson, will you pray this prayer with me? "Lord, I am amazed! You know all my faults and failures, and still You want to be close to me. There You stand, arms open wide. All I have to do is make the first move. Thank You, Lord, for your unfailing love. Amen."

Draw near to God, cleanse your hands and heart.
Read James 4:8.

1. Keeping in mind that James wrote to believers, what does his use of the word "sinners" in verse 8 imply?

2. (a) What must we do to sense God's presence in our lives?

   (b) How does a person draw near to God?

3. What does drawing near to God demand of us?

4. (a) "Cleanse your hands" has nothing to do with personal hygiene. What did dirty hands speak of to James's Jewish readers? Read Exodus 30:17–21 and Psalm 24:3 and 4.

(b) What do clean hands, clean heart and single-mindedness mean to you?

5. How does a double mind picture an unclean heart?

"The Devil will not get to you unless you get too far away from God. A wolf never attacks a sheep as long as it is with the rest of the sheep and with the shepherd. And the closer the sheep is to the shepherd, the safer it is. Our problem is that we get too far from God."[1]

Requirements for repentance
Read James 4:9.

6. What five injunctions are given in this verse?

(1)

(2)

(3)

(4)

(5)

7. These are not frivolous words, but, quite the contrast, severe words. Why must believers follow these directives?

Humility brings honor
Read James 4:10.

8. James pinpoints what we must do. What is it?

9. When James says, "Humble yourselves," what is he asking us to do?

"The way up is down. The lowly one becomes the lifted one. There is a marked advantage to humility—eventually it brings honor."[2]

---

10. What does it mean, in practical terms, for a humble backslider to be lifted up?

> *"The potter would sit at his work, turning the large stone wheel with his feet while shaping the clay on the small wooden wheel. . . . Spoiled, ruined, or marred vessels were not tossed aside and discarded in favor of those that emerged perfect. They were remade!"*[3]

Who made you a judge?
Read James 4:11 and 12.

11. Why did James mention evil speaking and judging immediately after describing how we can be made right before God?

> Tell not abroad another's faults
> Till thou hast cured thine own;
> Nor whisper of thy neighbor's sin
> Till thou art perfect grown:
> Then, when thy soul is pure enough
> To bear My searching eye
> Unshrinking, then may come the time
> Thy brother to decry.[4]

12. Give four reasons we should not speak evil of or judge a brother.

    (1)

    (2)

    (3)

    (4)

Are you wise enough to plan your life?
Read James 4:13–16.

13. James seems to be talking about humility again as he turns to the proud people who set themselves above providence and destiny. One commentator says verse 13 is "practical atheism." What do you think he means by that?

14. What decisive factor should we keep in mind in all our planning (verse 15)?

15. (a) Is James saying we should tack on "if it is the Lord's will" to every sentence?

    (b) What is he saying?

> *"We find the Christian life so difficult because we seek for God's blessing, while we live in our own will. We make our own plans and choose our own work, and then we ask Him to give us His blessing."* [5]

16. How is life like a vapor?

17. The ungodly not only plan their future without God, they even boast about it. What are the words you might hear coming from their lips?

You know what to do; will you do it?
Read James 4:17.

We have learned many ways to stretch our faith in these four chapters of James. What are we going to do with what we have learned?

18. Think back over the four chapters of James. List seven things you know God wants you to do.

    (1)

    (2)

    (3)

    (4)

    (5)

    (6)

    (7)

19. (a) Now that you know these things, what is your responsibility?

    (b) What is the result if you do nothing?

"People cannot become perfect by dint of [because of] hearing or reading about perfection. The chief thing is not to listen to yourself, but silently to listen to God. . . . You already know a great deal more than you practice. You do not need the acquirement of fresh knowledge half so much as to put in practice that which you already possess." [6]

 From My Heart

"Draw nigh to God, and he will draw nigh to you."

Sometimes I feel I am close to God, but I am not so sure He is close to me. Why? Because He seems to be sending things to hurt me instead of help me. Could the reason they hurt be because I don't want to accept them? I'm pulling away from them? I think so. Christ said, "My yoke is easy, and my burden is light" (Matthew 11:30). A yoke was used to keep cattle close together so they could work as one. So it is with Christ. If I accept His yoke, then it will be easy. But if I try to pull away from it, that's when it hurts. What is His yoke? Whatever He places on me to keep me close to Him so we can work as one.

"Draw nigh to God, and he will draw nigh to you."

Did you notice who has to make the first move? It is the same in staying close to Him. He tells us in Matthew 11:29, "Take my yoke upon you." Again, who must take the initiative to stay close? I must make the first move. After He places His yoke on me—and it is harder than I expected it to be—how will I respond? Will I accept it, or will I pull away and feel He is hurting me? Remember the words of Amy Carmichael: "In acceptance lieth peace" (p. 26).

"Lord, help me to remember I cannot draw close to You and pull away from You at the same time. Help me to accept Your yoke so I can stay close to You."

From Your Heart

Reflecting over this lesson, have you learned what it means to draw near to God? If you don't feel close to God, what can you do to change that?

Notes:

1. McGee, p. 662.

2. Walvoord & Zuck, p. 831.

3. Walter C. Kaiser, "Digging Deeper" (*Moody Monthly*, April 1991), p. 30.

4. Lyra Mystica, quoted by Tileston, p. 13.

5. M. J. Shepperson, compiler, *Day by Day with Andrew Murray* (Minneapolis: Bethany House Publishers, 1961), pp. 13, 14.

6. Francois de la Mothe Fenelon, quoted by Tileston, p. 171.

Stretched Faith Patiently Waits

JAMES 5:1–12

"Be ye also patient; stablish your hearts: for the coming of the Lord draweth nigh" (James 5:8).

James introduces chapter 5 with some harsh words to the wicked rich (5:1–6). Could he be speaking to the rich men mentioned in chapter 2, verses 6 and 7? Those rich people "despised the poor . . . oppress you, and draw you before the judgment seats."

In the next six verses (7–12) James comforts the brethren and encourages them to be patient, "for the coming of the Lord draweth nigh."

Before we start our study, will you pray this prayer with me? "Lord, You know how hard our journey here below can be. Help us to remember that when the way gets rough, it will be worth it someday! Just one glimpse of Your dear face, and all sorrows will be erased. Enable us to patiently run the race until we see You face to face. Amen."

The rich get richer.
Read James 5:1–3.

1. How do you define materialism?

2. Is James condemning these people for being rich or for being materialistic?

3. (a) How do these verses describe not only materialism but also excessive, extravagant living?

   (b) Describe this lifestyle in today's world.

   (c) How has your life been affected by materialism?

> Money is deceiving because it brings a false sense of security.
> Money can buy a bed, but it cannot give you rest.
> Money can buy food, but it can never satisfy the soul.
> Money can buy luxury, but it can never buy contentment.
> Money can buy stocks, but it can never give real security.
> Money can buy a house, but it cannot buy a home.
> Money can buy a church, but it can never buy a Savior.

4. What lessons are we to learn from verses 1–3?

The poor get poorer.
Read James 5:4–6.

5. The rich people James described were not only selfish and foolish but sinful and wicked as well. What were they doing to the poor (verse 4)?

6. These mistreated believers did not cry against their employers and take vengeance into their hands. What did they do?

7. The rich lived like greedy swine, nourishing their "hearts, as in the day of slaughter." What does verse 5 imply?

Be patient; the Lord is coming soon.
Read James 5:7 and 8.

8. (a) Instead of vengeance or retaliation, what did James urge the poor to do?

(b) Why?

> *"Live now as you shall have wished you lived when you stand at the judgment seat of Christ."*[1]

9. One of the most difficult things God asks us to do is be patient in the midst of trials. What are you experiencing (or have you experienced) that is stretching your faith and the only answer that comes from God is "be patient"?

10. "Stablish" in verse 8 means "strengthen." How can the hope of Christ's return strengthen our hearts?

> If we could see beyond today, as God can see,
> If all the clouds should roll away, the shadows flee;
> O'er present griefs we would not fret,
> Each sorrow we would soon forget;
> For many joys are waiting yet
> For you and me.

If we could see, if we could know, we often say.
But God in love a veil doth throw across our way.
We cannot see what lies before
And so we cling to Him the more,
He leads us till this life is o'er;
Trust and obey.[2]

Don't get impatient.
Read James 5:9.

11. Why are we prone to fall into grumbling, complaining, and judging one another when we're in the midst of a trial?

12. James spoke of judging one another in chapter 4; now he comments on God's judgment. What warning does God give us in regard to judging? Read Romans 14:10 and 13.

Examples of patience
Read James 5:10 and 11.

> "There are many things that God does not fix precisely because He loves us. *Instead of extracting us from the problem, . . . He calls—'This is a necessary part of the journey. Even if it is the roughest part, it is only a part, and it will not last the whole long way. Remember where I am leading you. Remember what you will find at the end—a home and a haven and a heaven.'* "[3]

13. "The Lord is very pitiful, and of tender mercy." What does this say to us in regard to suffering patiently? Read 1 Corinthians 10:13.

14. When we speak of trials and patience, what Old Testament saint usually comes to our minds?

15. Job endured much and was steadfast in his suffering. However, he was sometimes impatient with God (e.g., Job 10:1–10). How do we display our impatience with God when trials go on and on?

Mean what you say; say what you mean.
Read James 5:12.

James has been instructing believers to be patient in suffering. Now he reminds them to be patient and cautious with their speech.

> "Every man's heart is a storehouse, and his words show what he keeps there. What is said on the spur of the moment is sometimes better evidence of a man's disposition than what he says deliberately, for the latter many be calculated hypocrisy."[4]

16. The Jews were great at using various oaths to back up their statements, but they avoided using God's name lest they blaspheme Him. How does God feel about needless oaths and words?

17. What are some needless statements Christians make to emphasize yes or no?

18. (a) Look up "euphemism" in a dictionary and write the definition.

 (b) What euphemisms or "minced oaths" do some Christians use?

 (c) Look up "gee" and "gosh" in a dictionary to see what they stand for.

19. Verse 12 says, "Lest ye fall into condemnation." Many people will be ashamed when they stand before Christ (Matthew 12:36, 37; 1 John 2:28). Are you using words or minced oaths you need to correct? Write what they are and ask God to help you erase them from your vocabulary.

From My Heart

Do you like the word "wait"? Most of the time it irritates me because I'm usually in a hurry. Our society doesn't like to wait either. We want things fast, even instant, if possible. We live in the age of instant pudding, instant potatoes, micro-waveable meals, drive-up windows for banking and shopping, fax machines, and the list goes on and on.

Yet God tells us, "We count them happy which endure." And He doesn't just mean endure, but patiently endure. Wow! To be honest with you, I have a hard time patiently enduring suffering and trials; but I have learned one thing that makes it easier. When I start to get bogged down, I try to remember, "This may not last the whole way, but if it does, this is not my final home. I'm only passing through down here. Christ may come today, and then I'll be in my final Home, Heaven."

We can handle anything for one day—as long as we know it won't last forever. So keep looking up. Today may be our final day, and we'll go to our final Home, Heaven.

From Your Heart

Reflecting over this lesson, are you looking forward to Christ's return? When do you long for Heaven the most?

Notes:

1. William Culbertson, quoted by Norma Whitcomb and Frances Randall, *Food and Thought* (Grand Rapids: Baker Book House, 1973), p. 74.

2. Anonymous, quoted by Sweeting, pp. 138, 139.

3. Elliot, *Loneliness,* p. 89.

4. Alfred Plummer, quoted by Strauss, p. 199.

A Final Look at Afflictions

JAMES 5:13–20

"Is any among you afflicted? let him pray. Is any merry? let him sing psalms" (James 5:13).

James is about to end his letter, but I trust the impact of what we have learned will not end. He has covered many subjects and touched on just about every aspect of the Christian life in these five short chapters. He ends the book with another reminder about the importance of prayer and caring for one another.

Before we start this lesson, will you pray this prayer with me? "Lord, if my mouth could be continually filled with prayer and praise, my life would be continually filled with peace and joy. Oh, how I long for that! Remind me when worthless, hurtful things fill my heart and mind to replace them with prayer and praise. Lord, I humbly ask for Your grace and strength to do this. Amen."

When to pray and when to praise
Read James 5:13–15a.

1. What are two great weaknesses in the average Christian's life?

2. Why do people neglect the areas of prayer and praise?

3. Our natural response to affliction and suffering should be prayer. However, what do we usually do first?

The literal meaning of the word "affliction" is "to suffer the evil blows of the outside world."

4. Why does the Bible encourage us to pray when we are suffering and are in great turmoil?

   Psalm 50:15

   1 Peter 3:12

The original word for merry is *euthumei*. The word denotes a deep sense of well-being, not a superficial euphoria.

5. Why does the Bible encourage us to "sing psalms," or to praise the Lord, when things are going well?

   1 Chronicles 16:8–10

   Colossians 3:16 and 17

> In every joy that crowns my days,
> In every pain I bear,
> My heart shall find delight in praise,
> Or seek relief in prayer.[1]

In verses 13 and 14 James seems to be speaking to three groups of people:
   • Suffering ones (afflicted)—they need to pray.
   • Sufficient ones (merry)—they need to praise.
   • Sick ones (seriously ill)—they need special prayer.
(Bible scholars differ in their interpretations of verses 14 and 15. Some say "sick" refers to those who are weak, not necessarily those who are physically ill. Some say "sick" does refer to serious physical illness, and some say this sickness is because of sin, as in 1 Corinthians 11:30.)

6. (a) Does God intend to heal everyone?

   (b) How do these verses prove or disprove your answer?
       2 Timothy 4:20; Philippians 2:25–27; 2 Corinthians 12:7–
       10.

"God sometimes gives unexpected answers to our prayers. . . . For a long time God does not seem to answer at all. Then, when he does answer, what he says is even more mysterious than his apparent failure to listen to our prayers. . . . But Scripture teaches us that God sometimes answers our prayers by allowing things to become much worse before they become better. He may sometimes do the opposite of what we anticipate. . . . We must always be prepared for the unexpected when we are dealing with God."[2]

---

7. Paul asked three times to be healed. (a) Was the lack of
   healing due to a lack of faith?

   (b) What does 2 Corinthians 12:7–9 give as the reason?

"Why were some . . . heroes of faith delivered while others were tormented—because some had faith and others had none? No! They all had faith. They all believed in the same God, but God's will was not accomplished in the same way through them all."[3]

---

8. James did not say a sick person should call a "faith healer."
   Whom did he say to call?

9. When the elders arrived, what were they to do?

10. Oil was regarded as therapeutic in Bible times (e.g., Luke 10:34). We know the oil was not the main cause for healing. What was?

11. Some people assume healing is guaranteed by the words in verse 15, "the prayer of faith shall save the sick." Why didn't James add the qualifying statement, "if it be God's will"?

> "Sometimes we want things we were not meant to have. Because He loves us, the Father says no. Faith trusts that no. Faith is willing not to have what God is not willing to give. Furthermore, faith does not insist upon an explanation. It is enough to know his promise to give what is good—He knows so much more about that than we do."[4]

Confessing sins and faults

Read James 5:15b and 16a.

12. James realized the sick man might need to deal with another problem. What kind of healing did he speak of in verse 15b?

13. (a) To whom are we to confess our sins so that we might
        be forgiven? Read 1 John 1:9.

    (b) To whom are we to confess our faults when we have
        offended someone or are offended by someone?

Effective prayer
Read James 5:16b–18.

14. What kind of praying is effective? Read also Proverbs 15:29.

15. Review James 4:15. What should we keep in mind when we
    pray?

16. Why do you think James used the illustration of Elijah as
    an example of effective prayer (verses 17 and 18)?

Saving a brother
Read James 5:19 and 20.

    James has referred to the brethren almost twenty times,
and he ends the book with "brethren." He has taught his Christian brothers, scolded them, challenged them, and warned
them. Now he challenges and encourages them once again.
    The word "err" refers to wandering. It is not a sudden
thing, but like a slow drifting with the tide.

17. James does not say his readers have wandered away from the church, but from the "truth." Why is this so dangerous?

18. How can a fellow believer be the means of salvation ("converteth the sinner") for a backslidden brother in Christ? Read Galatians 6:1–4.

19. No matter how far a backslider goes, if he is still sensitive to his sin, he can be restored. What will God do with the multitude of his sins? Read Psalm 103:12.

> *"We need the tenderness of James for our brothers and sisters in Christ who have gone astray. Such passion will not permit us to gossip about them nor turn from them, but will contrariwise draw us to them in loving concern. Biblical Christianity has a message of divine love for the unsaved, but no stronger appeal will be made to those who are outside of Christ than to see Christians loving and restoring their own who have fallen. This is indeed the Spirit of our Lord Jesus Christ."[5]*

20. Have you ever wandered from the truth? How did it happen? Who helped bring you back? How would you go about helping someone else who has wandered from the truth?

From My Heart

James has taught me so much. I have clearly seen how I can achieve spiritual maturity. Spiritual maturity involves every aspect of my life, and James has touched on every area from trials to the tongue, from submission to the use of money, from Bible reading to criticism, from temptation to prayer. I don't think he missed anything. Now the question is, What will I do with all these things I have learned? I am reminded again of my verse for the year: "Be ye doers of the word, and not hearers only, deceiving your own selves" (James 1:22).

I am now responsible for even more truth than I was before. Will I daily weave these lessons into my life, or will I put my notebook away and say, "That was a good study"? I want to be a "doer" of the Word, and, by God's grace and with His help, I shall be. I must remember James 4:17: "Therefore to him that knoweth to do good, and doeth it not, to him it is sin."

I want to end this lesson series with a statement that I used to introduce it: "He [James] drew a vivid picture of what a Christian is like in his speech, actions, feelings and possessions. James will stretch our faith to its outer limits."

My faith has been stretched; has yours?

May God bless you and keep stretching your faith!

Juanita

From Your Heart

Reflecting over this lesson, how would you evaluate prayer and praise in your life? In which area do you need the most improvement?

Notes:

1. Strauss, p. 211.

2. D. Martyn Lloyd-Jones, *Faith Tried and Triumphant* (Grand Rapids: Baker Book House, 1987), pp. 10, 11.

3. George Sweeting, p. 153.

4. Elliot, *A Lamp for My Feet,* p. 52.

5. Strauss, p. 227.

LEADER'S GUIDE

SUGGESTIONS FOR LEADERS

The effectiveness of a group Bible study usually depends on two things: (1) the leader herself; and (2) the ladies' commitment to prepare beforehand and interact during the study. You cannot totally control the second factor, but you have total control over the first one. These brief suggestions will help you be an effective Bible study leader.

You will want to prepare each lesson a week in advance. During the week, read supplemental material. The books from which the quotations are taken and that are listed in the notes section of each lesson are good supplements, as are magazine articles and Bible commentaries. Look for illustrations in the everyday events of your life as well as in the lives of others.

Encourage the ladies in the Bible study to complete each lesson before the meeting itself. This will make the discussion more interesting. You can suggest that ladies answer two or three questions a day as part of their daily Bible reading time rather than trying to do the entire lesson at one sitting.

You may also want to encourage the ladies to memorize the key verse for each lesson. (This is the verse that is printed in italics at the start of each lesson.) If possible, print the verses on 3" x 5" cards to distribute each week. If you cannot do this, suggest that the ladies make their own cards and keep them in a prominent place throughout the week.

The physical setting in which you meet will have some bearing on the study itself. An informal circle of chairs, chairs around a table, someone's living room or family room—these types of settings encourage people to relax and participate. In addition to an informal setting, create an atmosphere in which ladies feel free to participate and be themselves.

During the discussion time, here are a few guidelines to observe:

• Don't do all the talking. This study is not designed to be a lecture.

• Encourage discussion on each question by adding ideas and questions.

• Don't discuss controversial issues that will divide the group. (Differences of opinion are healthy; divisions are not.)

• Don't allow one lady to dominate the discussion. Use statements such as these to draw others into the study: "Let's hear from someone on this side of the room" (the side opposite the dominant talker); "Let's hear from someone who has not shared yet today."

• Stay on the subject. The tendency toward tangents is always possible in a discussion. One of your responsibilities as the leader is to keep the group on the track.

• Don't get bogged down on a question that interests only one person.

You may want to use the last fifteen minutes of the scheduled time for prayer. If you have a large group of ladies, divide into smaller groups for prayer. You could call this the "Share and Care Time."

If you have a morning Bible study, encourage the ladies to go out for lunch with someone else from time to time. This is a good way to get acquainted with new ladies. Occasionally you could plan a time when ladies bring their own lunches or salads to share and have lunch together. These activities help promote fellowship and friendship in the group.

The formats that follow are suggestions only. You can plan your own format, use one of these or adapt one of these to your needs.

2-hour Bible Study

10:00—10:15	Coffee and fellowship time
10:15—10:30	Get-acquainted time
	Have two ladies take five minutes each to tell something about themselves and their families.
	Also use this time to make announcements and, if appropriate, take an offering for the baby-sitters.
10:30—11:45	Bible study
	Leader guides discussion of the questions in the day's lesson.
11:45—12:00	Prayer time

2-hour Bible Study

10:00—10:45	Bible lesson
	Leader teaches a lesson on the content of the material. No discussion during this time.
10:45—11:00	Coffee and fellowship
11:00—11:45	Discussion time
	Divide into small groups with an appointed leader for each group. Discuss the questions in the day's lesson.
11:45—12:00	Prayer time

1¹/₂-hour Bible Study

10:00—10:30	Bible study
	Leader guides discussion of half the questions in the day's lesson.
10:30—10:45	Coffee and fellowship
10:45—11:15	Bible study
	Leader continues discussion of the questions in the day's lesson.
11:15—11:30	Prayer time

ANSWERS FOR LEADER'S USE

Information inside parentheses () is additional instruction for the group leader.

LESSON 1

1. A servant of God and the Lord Jesus Christ.

2. Jesus and James's other brothers (Joses, Simon, Judas) and his sisters.

3. James is practicing what he preaches in James 4:10, humility. He placed himself on the same level as all of God's servants.

4. Name-drop.

5. It makes us feel more important and valuable. But God says we're valuable because of who we are—not who we know.

6. Being Christian Jews, they would be rejected by their own country-

men as well as by the Gentiles. Families were being separated and scattered. Some families may not have known where other family members were.

7. They would be scattered among all nations.

8. Count it all joy when trials come into your life.

9. Our first response is usually, "Why me?" Then we may ask, "Why now? Why this?" We're never ready for trials.

10. We think we deserve something better, and, in reality, we are questioning God's goodness and wisdom in allowing trials.

11. When you fall into a trial, evaluate—with joy—what you can learn from it.

12. Philippians 4:13—I can do anything with God's strength. Isaiah 40:31— "Renew" in this verse literally means "exchange." When I exchange my strength for God's strength, I can count it all joy. Isaiah 26:3—I keep reminding myself of God's promises and keep trusting Him to fulfill them in my life, and He gives peace.

13. (a) When. (b) (Have the ladies share some experiences in their lives.) (c) (Again, ask a few ladies to share their answers to this question.)

14. The trial is unexpected or unplanned.

15. *Divers*—of two kinds, diverse, various. *Temptations*—testings, trials. *Trying*—proving, testing. *Worketh*—develops. *Patience*—perseverance, steadfastness, endurance. *Perfect*—mature, finished. *Entire*—complete, fully developed.

16. My brothers in Christ, evaluate the experience as joyful when you encounter various trials because you know that you will develop perseverance when your faith is tested or proved. Perseverance, in turn, will cause you to mature and become fully developed.

17. Trials test our faith, and the end result will be patience to endure.

18. It would never be stretched or grow.

19. Mature ones.

20. (a) Spiritual. (b) As I mature spiritually, I will not lack anything I need spiritually to handle any situation I face.

LESSON 2

1. Two of our greatest needs are wisdom and faith.

2. We're often confused. We can't understand what God is doing, and we don't know how to handle what is happening. We need God's wisdom and guidance.

3. Our mates, families, friends, a pastor, or counselor.

4. God, the Wonderful Counselor.

5. (a) Generously, not grudgingly. (b) He just keeps giving.

6. He never says, "Why are you asking again?" He does not question or chide. His is a simple giving with no spirit of bitterness.

7. They don't ask in faith. When we don't trust God, we trust ourselves; then God can't work.

8. Like water being tossed to and fro by the wind.

9. One day we trust God, the next day we don't. There is never any peace because we are tossed about by doubt and fear.

10. Faith comes by hearing the Word of God. Practicing what we hear creates faith in our hearts.

11. A firm conviction that God loves me and is in control, when I can't see

or understand what He is doing. I also believe God is good even when things don't look good.

12. (a) The poor realize they are truly rich because they belong to Christ; in Heaven they will stand side by side with the rich. (b)The rich man understands his true wealth is not in material things but in his eternal riches. Externally these two are different; internally they are the same: they both need faith.

13. They are here today and gone tomorrow.

14. Endurance and love for God.

15. With a crown of life.

16. It could be both.

LESSON 3

1. When.

2. It starts from within, not without. It starts in our hearts when the sinful, lustful nature takes over.

3. (1) Lust (desire). (2) Drawn away (deception). (3) Conceive (Disobedience). (4) Finished (Death).

4. Sin brings death to relationships. Sin brings death to a reputation. Sin brings death to self-worth. The person lives a death experience similar to an unbeliever who is separated from God.

5. The sin starts in our hearts with lust, then lust conceives. Conception is the union of two. Our sinful, lustful nature joins with outward temptation, and sin is born. If sin completely takes over our lives, we lose communication with God. Our sin separates us from God, and our fellowship with Him is broken. Don't be led astray or deceived by sin; it is deadly.

6. (Have the ladies share some of the experiences they have had.)

7. When we remember how good God has been to us and all of the blessings He has given, how can we turn our backs on Him and deliberately sin? (Joseph said this in Genesis 39:9.)

8. God, Who gives good gifts, will keep doing it; He never changes.

9. Begat.

10. The Word of truth, the Bible.

11. (a) No. (b) God originates the birth, and it comes as a result of hearing the Word of truth.

12. Firstfruits were the first crops grown, given to God in their raw state (Exod. 22:29; 23:19). The New Testament uses the term to indicate abundance, excellence, a sample of the full harvest. James was saying believers were to give their best to God.

13. We are the best and the finest of His creation.

14. We are on display in this world to bring honor, not dishonor, to God.

15. The Word can point out the error of our way or keep us from error.

16. When we are enticed into sin, we often blame God or others. We don't want to hear what God's Word has to say, we argue with God or we even get angry with God.

17. Many times when God doesn't do what we think He should do, we get angry at Him. We begin to shout orders to our Commander, Who is in control of us. Many people who once had bright testimonies for God are now angry, bitter people. The world looks at them and calls them hypocrites.

18. Take out unclean thoughts and deeds ("filthiness and superfluity of naughtiness").

19. The Word of God must be planted, ingrown, or inborn into the soil of our souls if we are to keep ourselves from sin.

20. It can keep out lust from within and help us resist temptation from without. These things, if unchecked, lead to sin and death.

LESSON 4

1. God's Word.

2. It demands action! You can't passively read it and lay it down without being challenged to obey it.

3. It shows us what we really are (our sinful nature) and what we can become (Christlike).

4. He thinks he is saved because he goes to church and does some outward deeds, but he has no desire to please God. He doesn't even know that the reason he has no desire to please God is because he is not saved. Such a person is building on a false foundation.

5. We are only hearers of the Word, not doers. We may have a living faith in Christ but not a growing faith. A growing faith leads to action; it will be stretched. It will make us more than auditors; we will be conquerors.

6. It gives a reflection of ourselves and shows things that need to be done to look right and be right.

7. Many women spend a great deal of time covering up blemishes and making themselves look good outwardly. Few spend the same amount of time working on inward beauty by reading, obeying, and meditating on God's Word.

8. We might say she is careless or lazy.

9. (a) When we obey the Word and are right with God and others, we feel a freedom and peace in our hearts. (b) Disobedience brings us into the bondage of fear, guilt, shame, and turmoil.

10. The one who ignores, neglects or refuses to do what the Word requires.

11. (a) (Encourage the ladies to examine their hearts and answer this question.) (b) (Have a few ladies share their answers.)

12. Some people read the Bible and pray daily (the motions), but they lack the devotion to Christ that demands a changed life.

13. (a) Seem. (b) E.g., thinks himself.

14. The word has to do with going through a ritual, a form, or a ceremony.

15. The emphasis is on his outward performance rather than on his heart.

16. He seems to be religious; he does not bridle his tongue; he deceives himself.

17. He thinks outward performances alone please God.

18. (1) Self-control, a bridled tongue. (2) Love for others. (3) Holiness or purity.

19. *Bridled tongue*—We don't speak evil of others or use unbecoming language. *Love for others*—We are concerned about those in need, especially those who can give nothing in return (e.g., widows and orphans). *Holiness or purity*—We are being right not only outwardly but also inwardly. When we are right inwardly, the filth of this world does not appeal to us.

LESSON 5

1. Making unfair distinctions between people, or judging people by their outward appearance.

2. Faith judges on things not seen; favoritism judges on what can be seen.

3. Two visitors enter the church. One is wearing fine clothing and gold, the other man is obviously poor. The usher greets the rich man and leads him into the auditorium to a good seat. The poor man is left to find his own seat with no one to greet him and make him feel welcome.

4. Tennis shoes, jeans, and other items are more impressive if they have the right labels on them. Certain areas are known as *the* place to live. Particular brands of cars impress, and the name sounds plush.

5. We could be more interested in what they have than what they are. If we show special attention to them, it may benefit us materially. Since the poor can't do anything for us, we give to them, expecting nothing in return.

6. (a) No. (b) God does not choose on merit. He chose the weak to become witnesses, the foolish to be faithful, and the world's nobodies to be nobility.

7. (1) Don't the rich oppress and slander you? (2) Aren't the rich the ones who are dragging you into court? (3) Aren't they the ones who slander Jesus' noble name?

8. Showing love is obeying God. Having respect of persons is disobeying God.

9. (a) No. (b) They were familiar with the Old Testament law, and it was stated there.

10. Six commands (5–10) refer to how we should treat others.

11. It rules all other laws. There would be no need for most of the other laws if we kept this one.

12. How many laws must a man break before he is a lawbreaker? Just one! We all stand guilty before God as sinners in need of forgiveness.

13. Adultery and murder.

14. We are free to love others because Christ has set us free from our self-centeredness, prejudice, hate, and bitterness.

15. If we're not showing mercy, we will not receive mercy from man or God, here or at the Judgment Seat. See Matthew 5:7.

16. (Ask the ladies to take time to examine their hearts.)

17. (Ask the ladies to share examples of how we show favoritism.)

LESSON 6

1. Saving faith is a living faith; professing faith is a dead faith

2. Faith.

3. They have done "religious" things and have done them in God's name.

4. We were saved to serve—"created . . . unto good works." We serve out of gratitude because we *are* saved, not to get saved or to keep saved.

5. A dead faith with no evidence of reality in it. There are many professors of faith in Christ, but few real possessors.

6. (a) No, this would be impossible. (b) He is illustrating that words without deeds are of no value to the needy. Likewise, words without acts of faith will profit us nothing with God.

7. We will see growth and fruit. It will also be a place of shelter and refuge.

A bird never builds a refuge in a dead tree.

8. His life is unproductive and barren. We never see change or growth.

9. (a) None that I know of. (b) There is nothing else; all we have is our fruit. "By their fruits ye shall know them" (Matt. 7:20). We don't have to guess if a tree is alive. Its fruitful—or unfruitful—condition gives the answer. In the same way, living faith produces the evidence of faith: good works.

10. I can say anything with my mouth, and it may not be true. However, if my heart has been changed by the new birth, how I live will demonstrate what I speak. "For out of the abundance of the heart the mouth speaketh" (Matt. 12:34).

11. Demons.

12. Mark 3:11—The deity of Christ. Luke 8:29–31—The existence of a place of punishment.

13. A person whose words are empty; he talks much but says little. Writer John Blanchard calls him a "spiritually ignorant windbag."

14. Faith that works.

15. (a) No; he was already justified by his belief in God's promise in Genesis 15:4–6. (b) No; Abraham raised the knife to offer Isaac, but he did not have to put him to death as a sacrifice. (c) He believed God would raise Isaac from the dead.

16. Even the lowest and poorest of people must demonstrate works as evidence of genuine faith.

17. We would be vain and boastful if we could save ourselves. It is all of faith plus nothing.

18. We are saved by faith, but works show we have a living faith. Works show our "vital signs" are functioning and tell how we are doing spiritually.

(If the ladies have not thought about the "spiritual check-up," ask them to do so now. You may want to ask a few ladies to share their answers if time allows.)

LESSON 7

1. It is a great responsibility to be a teacher. If we don't know or tell the truth, we could lead people astray. The teacher has the power of truth or error.

2. We all stumble and fall, but we must be always aiming at maturity and Christlikeness. Christ was the only One Who never offended with His tongue. God wants us to become more like Christ, not offending and condemning with our tongues.

3. When we begin to see a difference in how we are able to control our tongues, we know we are making progress spiritually; we're beginning to mature.

4. A small bit controls the whole body of a horse. A small rudder controls a great ship.

5. It has the power to control and direct our lives and the lives of others.

6. When my tongue is out of control, it raises my blood pressure, gives me headaches, puts knots in my stomach, and makes me ugly.

7. I can intimidate others; I can be so critical and condemning that people feel uncomfortable around me; I can make others feel worthless and unloved.

8. Good—If I see a brother beginning to slip spiritually and I lovingly

share with him my concern, I may save him from spiritual destruction. Nathan did this for David (2 Sam. 12:1–7). Evil—I can turn a person against another brother by sharing a secret fault he has. He may have a hard time forgetting what I tell him and even tell someone else. The first person's reputation may eventually be ruined because of my evil tongue.

9. Fire under control is a source of worth and help; a Spirit-controlled tongue is a source of blessing and encouragement. Uncontrolled fire is devastating and can do inestimable damage; an uncontrolled tongue can devastate a person and do irreparable damage. Words once spoken can never be called back.

10. (Have the ladies share circumstances they were involved in or know of.)

11. In order to keep our relationship right with God, we must keep our relationship with others right as well.

12. The picture is one of great variety and vastness, suggesting that the tongue is capable of committing every sin known to man.

13. The mouth speaks what is in a person's heart, and the evil he speaks with his tongue spots or stains (defiles) his entire person.

14. One uncontrolled tongue can defile and destroy the whole body of believers in a local assembly.

15. (a) Not necessarily; however there should be a difference if a person has been growing spiritually. (b) The tongue can never be perfectly controlled at all times because the tongue is like a smoldering fire, with sparks that can ignite at any time.

16. When anger and hate control our tongues, this is of the Devil and not from the Spirit of God. Man cannot control demon power; only God can.

17. Unruly evil—No one can ever be sure he will not have a slip of the tongue and say the wrong thing. Who can honestly say, "I will never say an unkind or critical thing again?" No one! Full of deadly poison—The tongue, like poison, can destroy a person instantly or slowly and secretly; a word here, a word there until the person is destroyed.

18. With God's help, I can control what I say.

LESSON 8

1. He speaks pious words at church and pitiful ones at home.

2. Continually condemn, criticize, and tear down another until she feels worthless, useless, and unloved.

3. We may not really belong to God. We may be like the religious man in James 1:26.

4. A person who plays two parts. Years ago an actor would put on two different masks, one to play the good guy and the other to play the bad guy.

5. The real can't do what is unreal. A fountain cannot give sweet and bitter water, just as a fig tree cannot produce figs and olives.

6. We must have a personal relationship with Jesus Christ so the Holy Spirit can control us. We must then let the Holy Spirit have full control of us so our old sinful nature does not control us.

7. Envy and strife.

8. Envy and strife produce arrogance and boasting as well as self-deception. We are so deceived we begin to lie to ourselves.

9. Jealousy.

10. Jealousy will drive people to do anything necessary to get what they want, no matter how much strife and turmoil it causes them or others.

11. Earthly—Seeks man's guidance, not God's. Sensual—Does his own thing, no matter where it leads, disregarding God or man. Devilish—Is evil and controlled by Satan.

12. Confusion and every evil work.

13. God is not the author of confusion but of peace.

14. It comes from our Heavenly Father.

15. Our lives are characterized by a gentle, humble spirit.

16. Christ.

17. Christ did not retaliate and give insult for insult or anger for anger; He committed His cause to God, knowing He was in control.

18. *Pure*—Undivided, blameless, consecrated, holy. God's wisdom starts with an undivided heart, devoted to Him. When purity characterizes us, people can see in our lives and hear in our speech all the following qualities. *Peaceable*—Peace-loving, quietness, rest. God's wisdom produces quiet and peaceable words in us. If we are walking in peace with God, we will be peaceable with those around us. *Gentle*—Mild, patient. God's wisdom directs our speech in a mild and patient manner with others, overlooking their weaknesses. *Easy to be entreated*—Trust, yield. Our words demonstrate a willingness to listen to others and trust them, even yielding to their view. *Full of mercy*—Compassion. God's wisdom allows us to speak compassionate words to those who wrong us. *Good fruits*—Good deeds. God's wisdom produces good works in our lives and speech. *Without partiality*—Does not discriminate. God's wisdom allows us to speak of others without judging and showing favoritism. *Without hypocrisy*—Without pretense. God's wisdom does not cover up; it is unmasked and totally honest in everything.

19. (Encourage the ladies to take a minute and score themselves if they have not already done this. You might want a few of the ladies to share their answers to the second part of the question.)

20. Sow peace.

LESSON 9

1. There was much hostility and verbal abuse taking place.

2. Inner lusts and desires.

3. People and circumstances.

4. People will be contentious and critical, tearing down one another to fulfill their own evil desires.

5. (a) Selfishness. (b) (Ask the ladies to take a few minutes to examine their lives.)

6. With his tongue. The tongue can destroy a home, a reputation, or a person's spirit. These are only a few things; the list could go on and on.

7. (a) Carnality or worldliness. (b) (Again, ask the ladies to examine their hearts.)

8. Prayerlessness—"ye ask not"—and selfish praying—"that ye consume it on your own lusts."

9. They are too busy scheming and manipulating to get whatever it is they want.

10. Selfish; they want their own way.

11. It would keep us from praying for things to satisfy our old, sinful nature.

12. Asking according to God's will; wanting what He wants for me, not what I want.

13. (a) He calls them adulterers and adulteresses. (b) They appear to be worldly, backslidden Christians.

14. The actions described in 4:4 demonstrate earthly, sensual, devilish wisdom rather than heavenly wisdom.

15. When we receive Christ as Savior, we come into a personal relationship with Him. The Bible pictures Christ as the husband and believers as the bride.

16. He turns from Christ and fulfills his lustful desires in the world. He looks to what the world has to offer—money, fame, pleasure—for satisfaction rather than seeking the riches that are in Christ.

17. (a) Unmerited favor. We give our worst to God, and He gives us His best. (b) It is given to those who humble themselves and acknowledge they need it.

18. Resist us, or bring whatever is needed into our lives to break our pride.

19. Submit ourselves to God and resist the Devil.

20. (a) Stand against him. (b) We face him head on in the power and might of the Lord and with our spiritual armor in place.

LESSON 10

1. James's readers were not living up to God's expectations of them.

2. (a) Draw near to Him. (b) A person can practice the presence of God in her life if she daily meditates on God's Word and obeys it. Practicing the presence of God also involves communion with God in prayer.

3. Clean hands, clean heart, and single-mindedness.

4. (a) The Old Testament priests had to wash their hands before offering sacrifices in the tabernacle or temple. This illustrated that no one could enter God's presence with dirty hands; that is to say, unconfessed sin. (b) Clean hands—confessed sin; clean heart—right motives; single-mindedness—correct focus and priorities.

5. "Double-minded" in the Greek means "having two souls." A believer who is torn between God and the world is double-minded. The world must be rooted out and the heart cleansed and consecrated totally for God.

6. (1) Be afflicted. (2) Mourn. (3) Weep. (4) Turn laughter to mourning. (5) Turn joy to heaviness.

7. If repentance is real, the sinner will see himself as God sees him and weep. He will not approach God carelessly.

8. Humble ourselves.

9. Admit we are wrong and change our behavior, which is the essence of repentance.

10. He will sense God's and man's forgiveness so he can face life again, free from his sin and guilt.

11. As soon as we begin to slip from God, judging and a critical spirit will come into our lives.

12. (1) He is a brother. (2) When we speak evil against a brother, we break the "royal law" (James 2:8): "Thou shalt love thy neighbour as thyself." (3)

God's law is not given for our opinion, but for our obedience. (4) Because God has unlimited knowledge, He has the authority and ability to judge all things. We don't have that ability; our judgment may be wrong.

13. Living without any regard to God's sovereignty and plan for our lives.

14. God's will. Our lives and our plans depend on God.

15. (a) No. (b) It is an attitude of submission to God's plans for our lives; we must want what He wants for our lives.

16. It is uncertain, transient, and temporary.

17. "I don't need God; I am the master of my fate."

18. (1) Count it all joy when trials come. (2) Don't let Satan deceive me and entice me into sin. (3) Don't show favoritism. (4) Produce good works in my life through faith. (5) Learn to control my tongue. (6) Loosen my grip on worldliness by having a submissive, humble spirit. (7) If I draw near to God, He will draw near to me.

19. (a) Obey them. (b) It is sin: "To him that knoweth to do good, and doeth it not, to him it is sin" (4:17).

LESSON 11

1. Over-emphasis or attention on material objects and needs with a disinterest in, or rejection of, spiritual values.

2. Materialistic.

3. (a) The rich had more than they could use. Perishable things were spoiling. Their closets bulged with more things than they could wear; their clothes were moth-eaten and ruined, but they had never been used. They were hoarding their money; the gold and silver were tarnishing and rusting. (b) (Have ladies share examples.) (c) (Allow time for ladies to think about this question. You may want to point out that even poor people can be materialistic.

4. We must not selfishly hoard everything we have when others have needs.

5. They were cheating the poor laborers and not giving them a fair day's wage.

6. They cried out to the Lord.

7. They did not realize a day of judgment was coming.

8. (a) Be patient and endure. (b) The Lord is coming soon.

9. (Ask a few ladies to share their experiences.)

10. The trial will be over when Christ returns.

11. We want to blame someone for our misery rather than submit to God and acknowledge He is in control; He has allowed the trial.

12. Judge ourselves! One day each of us will give an account of our own life—not someone else's.

13. God will never give us more trials than we can handle with His help.

14. Job.

15. We ask why. We may bargain with God and say, "I'll do this if You'll do this, God." Sometimes we put out the fleece (a reference to Gideon; see Judges 6:36–40).

16. Christians are not to use them. We should say what we mean. If we mean yes, we should say yes. If we mean no, we should say no.

17. "I'm telling the truth, so help me God." "I swear on a stack of Bibles."

18. (a) A word or phrase that is less distasteful than another. (b) Gee,

gosh, heck, doggone. (c) Gee—Jesus; gosh—God.

19. (Encourage the ladies to use this as a time of self-examination if they have not already done so.)

LESSON 12

1. Lack of prayer and failure to praise.

2. We have an enemy who doesn't want us to live victoriously. He knows prayer and praise are two essentials for a victorious life, so he does everything to divert our attention to other areas. Also, many Christians neglect these areas because they do not walk close to Christ.

3. Worry, complain, and tell everyone but God about our problems.

4. Psalm 50:15—When we call on the Lord, He will deliver us. 1 Peter 3:12—The Lord sees what is happening, and He listens to our prayers.

5. 1 Chronicles 16:8–10—We are to tell others how great our God is. Colossians 3:16 and 17—Singing is a way of expressing our gratitude to God for His goodness.

6. (a) No. (b) Paul had apostolic powers, but he did not heal Trophimus and Epaphroditus, his fellow-workers. Paul himself asked three times to be healed, but he was not.

7. (a) No. (b) Paul was not healed so God's power could be demonstrated through his weakness.

8. The elders of the church.

9. Pray and anoint the individual with oil.

10. The oil had no curative power. It could have been used as a means to provide comfort. It was the prayer of faith that resulted in healing.

11. James had already addressed this subject in 4:15—"For that ye ought to say, If the Lord will, we shall live, and do this, or that." James seems to take it for granted that his readers know their prayers are subject to the will and wisdom of a sovereign God.

12. Spiritual healing.

13. (a) God. (b) To the one we offended or to the one who offends us.

14. The fervent prayer of a righteous man.

15. Pray for God's will to be done.

16. Elijah was human just as we are. He was capable of becoming discouraged (1 Kings 19:1–18), but he also had faith to believe God could answer prayer (1 Kings 17:21, 22; 18:36–38).

17. We can justify any sin if we turn our backs on Christ and His Word; they both are truth (John 14:6; 17:17).

18. The most miserable person alive is a backslidden Christian who still feels the guilt and shame of his sin; he is existing in a death-like condition. The person who brings him back saves him from total spiritual destruction and from dying under divine discipline (Heb. 10:26, 27).

19. God hides them or covers them.

20. (If time allows, encourage a few ladies to share how God worked in their lives.)